M000280377

Copyright (c) 2014:

ISBN # 978-0-9964999-1-0

Contact Information:

Make Checks Payable To:
AC2BTG Publishing LLC
P.O. Box 78
Mullins SC 29574

Printed in the U.S.A

THE ART OF WINNING LITIGATION

BY: ERIC VAN BUREN

The Five Mind States

— "The probability of uncertainty dictates and

consumes our lives . "

--Schrodinger

— "Man's greatest foe is doubt."

--Unknown

— "There is no better than, or better at , there

is merely the skilled and unskilled, learned and

unlearned, practiced and unpracticed."

--Unknown

— "Among five kinds of warfare , war for justice and

war for defense are used by noble men. War out of

anger, war out of pride and war out of greed ...

are used by small men."

--Kaibara Ekken

— "The source of suffering is ego, the thought of

self. To know this is reason ... people without

reason don't understand the source of misery and

happiness; people without a sense of duty cannot

break the bonds of life and death."

--Suzuki Shosan

Introduction

"Bunbu Itchi"

In THE ART of winning litigation, the pen is never mightier than the sword. This is because your mind is the sword in THE ART of winning litigation and your mind and pen must be, as one, in accord. When this happens, so is Bunbu Itchi.

To embrace THE WAY of winning litigation, you must follow these very simple 9 rules:

- Do not think dishonestly
- THE WAY is training
- Become acquainted with every art associated with litigating
- Know the ways of all professions relevant to your litigation
- Distinguish between gain and loss in legal matters
- Develop intuitive judgment and understanding for everything
- Perceive those things which cannot be seen
- Pay attention, even to trifles
- Do nothing which is of no use when litigating

Preface

I am writing this manual at the beginning stages of my mastery in THE ART of winning litigation. I received my transmission through the Grandmaster Minkah Norwood.

The following transmission is for the beginner, the adept, the masters, and those who believe they are grandmasters.

Be guided by your own enlightenment. Fear nothing, but do not move in the absence of knowing or in the absence of being.

As I give this to you, once a master, you must relinquish this transmission pursuant to your own enlightenment.

In the third month, the third day, of the two thousand thirteen cycle.

About This Manual

I do not write touting my several legal victories or defeats. I do not write for literary acclamation or monetary gain. I write to relinquish and discharge my duty to those who seek truth in THE ART of winning litigation.

If you fear litigation, but must enter the arena, this manual is for you. If you are a law student serious about a career in litigation, this manual is for you. If you lose a litigation or have lost significantly in trial or other proceedings, this manual is for you. If law seems outside your mental and financial means, this manual is for you.

This manual does not teach you, it trains you and conditions you to receive the blessing of enlightenment. I am not a teacher, THE ART itself is that, I am and this manual is a guide. The revelation revealed to me through my enlightenment of THE ART of winning litigation is all I share.

There are several books you must read to receive my state of enlightenment. I will mention those pivotal to my mastery of this art; however, you must seek your own path to fulfill this transmission. This manual will achieve that task.

Proof

To prove the effectiveness of this manual to all litigants, from the partner in the powerful law firm, to the wary civil litigant looking for a lawyer to represent their action, to the lowest of the low of all litigants — the pro se criminal litigant. I have written this manual from the perspective and situation of the lowest litigant — the pro se criminal litigant.

The pro se criminal litigant is at the greatest initial disadvantage of any litigant. S/he is like a knife thrower pitted often against a machine gun wielding adversary. Most often, pro se criminal litigants are uneducated, mentally and/or emotionally challenged and/or unstable and indigent. When these factors exist, discipline and decorum are most often lacking.

Without discipline, how does one obtain victory? When I was in the infantile stages of receiving this transmission, I was conditioned to submit to the will of "THE WAY." Discipline was merely a subpart of that submission and came easily as a result. This manual is written using the predicament of the pro se litigant; however, it is written for every litigant and will condition them to submit to the will of THE WAY of winning litigation. However, one must take this manual seriously to receive enlightenment and mastery.

Table of Contents

Book I

Placebo:

Preparation administered like medicine but having no
physiological effect, prescribed for psychological
reasons or in a test

—The American

Century Dictionary

Book I

Advantage

In the first paragraph at the start of each book, I will cite texts that are not of a legal nature per se. They are mandatory if you want to gain the same enlightenment and mastery as I have of THE ART to winning litigation.

For this book, I cite with much earnest Nicomachean Ethics by Aristotle, The Book of 5 Rings (Gorin No Sho) and The Art of Strategy by R.L. Wang. These are the core books you must read to fully receive the full transmission of this entire text. If you can't afford any other books cited, you must find these before you finish reading this entire manual. I will cite them heavily.

The Body of Law

The body of law is like your own body. It must not be overworked or abused. Learning, researching, and deciphering and discussing law cannot be done all day. It is as extreme as weight lifting or training. I've found 2 hours with a 4 hour break in between sufficient. I would advise against engaging in law more than 6 hours a day until you become a master. Do not deviate from this lesson.

A Rock in the Water

Many times I have witnessed those who delve in the field of litigation tout years of experience. This is a critical thinking error. Years studying litigation the wrong way aids in your defeats. Some rocks sit in the water for years and if broken open will be dry on the inside. When we are taught in error, we think in error.

When we think in error, we act in error. The ultimate result is erroneous. Reflect on this profoundly.

Ethics

The ethics of THE ART of winning litigation are simple, one who is by nature bad cannot fully possess THE ART of winning litigation. We are by nature good or bad. Our deeds do not dictate who we are. Good people do bad things, and bad people do good things.

If you are bad by nature — like Darth Vader — you will receive enlightenment from the "dark force" (not THE ART of winning litigation).

Anger, pride, bias, deceit, entitlement, malice and hate distort our ability to win. We must not hate or dislike our adversary; however, during a challenge we must defeat our adversary through victory most often using its own treacherous tactics. The end and means must be situational based and balanced.

— See Nicomachean Ethics by Aristotle.

These are the proper ethics of THE ART.

Musashi

The sword saint of the Book of 5 Rings, also known as the Gorin No Sho, was a tactician of the highest form. It is written he won 60 duels to the death in his pursuit of understanding and mastering strategy.

The perfection of this understanding resulted in his grand mastery and enlightenment. He preached the daily study of THE ART of the sword.

3

Practice, upon practice, upon even more practice.

The ultimate realization of this result is that even the best knife thrower cannot beat an unskilled dummy with a machine gun; unless they understand that they must plan, strategize and practice how to defeat their opponent; before their opponent becomes an opponent.

You must at this point in this manual grow, accept and practice the warriors mind set, where it is believed to be an honor to die in the arena. Even and especially at the hands of your adversary.

It is the respect for THE GREAT ART that will propel you and the belief that there is no such belief as, better than or greater than, or more than you. In your mind there is only a belief of practiced or unpracticed, trained or untrained, skilled or unskilled; nothing else exists. When you condition your mind to accept this as truth; you will begin to see that there is always a way to victory. However, although you can die on the battle field honorably; when practicing THE ART of winning litigation, you cannot lose honorably.

— See The Gorin No Sho by Myomoto Musashi.

THE WAY

There are numerous ways to failure and only one way to victory. You must believe when victory is obtained, THE WAY victory was obtained is the only way the victory could have been obtained. Although there may have been many other ways to defeat the opponent, it doesn't matter, victory was obtained.

There are incalculable variables to each conflict, an inaudible rhythm to each contest; if you win by a lot or by a slim margin, it does not matter. The only thing that matters is you followed THE WAY to victory.

Do not be deceived that if you did this or that it would have improved your margin of victory. THE WAY is victory and you can only experience victory through THE WAY. You must be completely submissive to the will of THE WAY to be victorious. Reflect this profoundly.

The Advantage

Without employing THE WAY, you will have no advantage. And you will lose. When you are a master at throwing knives, and when your adversary has a machine gun, you will not win without the advantage. Knowing how and when to take the advantage in every situation in litigation is the only way to victory.

At times in litigation, we are throwing knives at machine gun wielders. When you become immune to dying on the battle field, and not through ignorance, you will find it easy to stand against a machine gun when you only wield a knife because you will be sure you have or know how to gain the advantage.

— See The Art of Strategy by R.L. Wang.

5 C's

Convivial, clever, cunning, contriving, and contingent. 5 C's that supersede knowledge. The

5C's that supersede knowledge IQ. or superior intellect.

Every warrior is built different. Some stronger, faster, more flexible, taller, smarter. However, when you litigate having low comprehension or IQ. or intelligence or threshold of focus, you must employ the 5 C's.

THE WAY doesn't care if you are brilliant or have an IQ. of 130, most of those with these traits believe they do not need to employ THE WAY. Sure they may occasionally find victory, but they will not follow it. A significant difference

Be honest with yourself, if you don't have a GED, you haven't conditioned yourself to litigate. If this is you, do not be discouraged. You must first look up each meaning of the 5 C's. Study and master them first. Employ them to learn and to assist in your learning of litigation techniques and procedures. THE GREAT ART will do the rest.

You Are

You are what you indulge in, read and watch. Scientific study has shown how reading comics every day for a month can significantly lower the comprehension of one reading on a collegiate level. Similar to weight training, once you stop lifting, you lose strength rapidly.

When I first opened a law book, I fell asleep. And I have a high IQ. I immediately cut out fictional novels and television. I only allowed myself to watch 3 hours of television a week, and I only read the books I cite in this manual.

Because I was undisciplined, I read slowly, very slowly at first. Later, I read to understand the gist of the text. Then I read separating the substance of each text. Then I read for the full understanding of each text. I ultimately learned every text is different.

It may take you days to understand something very simple, or minutes to understand what others believe is complex. This is the process of enlightenment.

When you fully understand a thing, you can tell others in simple terms to make them understand, especially if they do not know about litigation. This is when you know you fully understand a text or issue or claim or argument. THE WAY will garner enlightenment. Submit to its will.

The Courts

The courts in every litigating arena, are liken to a house hold. Imagine being the youngest in the household. You have an older sibling and then mom and dad. There are rights, rules, laws and procedure in this household that everyone must adhere to. When you have a gripe procedure states you bring it to the attention of your older sibling, then mom and then dad. So when there is a controversy — and there must be a controversy[1]— to forward your case procedurally — you bring it to court.

Let's say, the case you make is, the law says (which is posted on the refrigerator) I have a right that when I finish my homework, I can go outside and play. You present your finished homework as

---

[1] Neveres v.San Marcus Consol. Ind. Sch. Dist., 111 F. 3d 25, 26 (5th Cir. 1997)

evidence and argue the law. Your sibling challenges your evidence stating your homework is not done until it's correctly done. It's not correctly done, so you lose, but you appeal to your mom, as per the rule.

You argue the law again, and your mom is more concerned about your sibling's ruling than your evidence. Because there is a rule (not written on the refrigerator) practiced in this household that your homework must be correct. So your mom reviews the rule, your sibling's discretion in making her ruling, and you lose again. So you appeal again, to your father.

Your father is only concerned about what is stated on the refrigerator because the law does state that when you finish your homework, you can go outside and play. So your dad analyzes the law, the rule used by your sibling and mom against your right to go outside and play. Your dad rules your mom was correct in her ruling that your sibling used the right discretion in her ruling because the rule they used did not infringe upon your right to play.

In litigation, and as you can see we all endeavor in litigation in some form, the court that hears the case in controversy is always the first court you attend. If you lose, although you don't have a constitutional right to appeal[2], there most likely is a statutory right to appeal[3]. Appellate availability is usually available in internal hearings in institutions, agencies, corporations, organizations, and governments, as well.

---

[2] Abney v. Unite States, 431 U.S. 651, 656 (1977).
[3] Unites States v. Melancon, 972 F. 2d 566, 567 (5th Cir. 1992)

Trial Court (Sibling)

If you're a pro se litigant in the criminal arena, the trial court is the first court you attend. The trial court is where you argue facts. All admissible evidence is fact. However, evidence can be impeached, and considered for its trustworthiness when it is offered for truth. Credibility is usually what jurors use to give more or less weight to a specific piece of evidence. The Rules of Evidence determine if or how much of a specific piece of evidence can be used and the Rules of Procedure determine what procedures need to be followed to allow and govern aspects of the trial proceeding.

Appeals Court (Mother)

The next court for a pro se litigant if its case is not proven or sometimes even if it is; is the court of appeals. The court of appeals does not consider issues of credibility[4] and only looks to see if you received a fair trial.[5] The appeals court has specific procedures you must follow[6] and precedent it must follow.[7] There are certain rules that it's privy to[8] that the trial court is not.[9] It also allows for rehearing[10] by the 3 judge panel that reviews your case or from the entire panel of appellate judges in your circuit.

U.S. Supreme Court (Father)

If you lose your appeal (in federal court), the U.S. Supreme Court is available. The Supreme Court has its own specific rules and procedures you must follow.[11] Any issue you have you must

---

[4] Glasser v. United States, 315 U.S. 60, 80 (1942); United States v. Burgos, 94 F.3d 849, 863 (4th Cir . 1996)(en banc)
[5] Glasser v. United States, 315 U.S. 60, 80 (1942); United States v. Burgos, 94 F.3d 849, 863 (4th Cir. 1996)(en banc)
[6] Kaseman v. District of Columbia, 368 F.Supp.2d 27, 29 n. 1 (D.D.C. 2003).
[7] Parklane Hosiery Co. v. Shore, 439 U.S. 322, 326 (1979) (res judicata); United States v. Carter, 752 F.3d 8, 21 (1st Cir. 2014) (precedent).
[8] United States v. Robinson, 460 F.3d 550 (4th Circ. 2006).
[9] United States v. Cotton, 535 U.S. 625 (2002); United States V. Robinson, 460 F.3d 550 (4th Circ. 2006).
[10] United States v. Rosciano, 499 F.2d 173 (7th Circ. 1974) (per curiam).
[11] United States v. Wampler, 624 F.3d 1330 (10th Cir. 2010).

pose as a question which effects more than just your specific case. This question must ultimately effect the Constitution in some way.

Nine justices usually hear your case, and give a majority opinion[12] or per curiam opinions,[13] plurality opinions,[14] and/or dissenting opinions, and/or concurring opinions.[15] It also offers rehearing.

Post - Litigation

If you are unsuccessful in the Supreme Court, then you resort to post - litigation. If you're a pro se litigant in the criminal arena, the AEDPA[16]allows you 1 year from the date your Supreme Court certiorari was denied to file a petition attacking and/or challenging your conviction and/or sentence in the trial court. The species of this petition is uncertain.[17] However, it has specific procedures and rules you must follow.[18]

Must Know

What you must know in THE ART of winning litigation, is that the rules and procedures govern your situation. If you do not know them intimately, you will lose. The initiative most often lies within the rules and procedures. See Advantage.

— See The Gorin No Sho by Myomoto Musashi.
— See The Art of Strategy by R.L. Wang.
Your procedural posture is very important, liken to your heart when litigating. You have to know and learn all the rules and procedures of the court you attend. If you don't you will lose.

---

[12] Citizens United v. FEC, 558 U.S. 310, 447-60 (2010) (majority opinion).
[13] Mooney v. Holohan, 294 U.S. 103, 110 (1935) (per curiam).
[14] Freeman v. U n i t e d States, 131 S.Ct. 2685, 2690 (2011) (plurality opinion).
[15] Apprendi v. New Jersey, 530 U.S. 466, 523-54 (2000) (dissenting opinion.
[16] Raineri v. United States, 233 F.3d 96, 97 (1st Cir.2000) (AEDPA); Woodfurd v. Ngo, 126 S.Ct. 2378 (2006) (PLRA); Hughes v. United States, 263 F.3d 272 (3rd Cir. 2001) (FTCA).
[17] Mayle v. Felix, 545 U.S. 644 (2005).
[18] Clay V. United States, 537 U.S. 522, 525 (2003) (after certiorari); Mosier v. United States, 402 F.3d 116, 118 (2nd Cir.2005) (no appeal); United States v. Hadden, 475 F.3d 652 (4th Cir. 2007) (after resentencing).

Thesis, Antithesis, Synthesis:

And what is your name?

But I have no name.

Where is it? Have you lost it?

I can't remember.

Aaah you have misplaced it?

I don't recall.

If you have no name, what good is your word?

But I have no word.

You have no word? Then what will you do if someone asks for it?

Well, I haven't thought of it.

Was your name good or bad when you last seen it?

I believe it was good. A bad name is like no name.

You believe or you know?

Oh, I know.

And your word, was it good as well?

Oh yes indeed. I t was good because of my name.

And they are both lost?

Indeed.

Well if you can't give me your name or word why are we speaking?

Book II

Advantage

Before you finish Book II, you should read the book The Art of Thinking by Allen F. Harrison. This book will not only show you how you think, it will show you how others think. It is essential that you understand how you think when you litigate so you can prepare correctly against your adversary. I also urge you to read Uncommon Sense: A Convict's Guide to the Law by Timothy Dale Crockett. Although testy, it is vigilant as you should always be.

The books I cite under the Advantage section at the beginning of each book should not be read hurriedly. As you read and reread them, you will gain different levels of enlightenment. As with this manual, each reading will provide you with a more clear and profound understanding of how to perfect winning litigation. The parts of this manual which seem rudimentary or insignificant upon first reading, will induce profound enlightenment in a latter reading. As well, some parts of this manual which seem opaque, will become clear in a latter reading. You must read these books deliberately and diligently.

Your Name/Word

In the discourse at the beginning of Book II, I ask you as a litigant: What does it mean? Is it a simple discourse? Is it an argument? Is there a thesis? An antithesis? Is there some synthesis? In litigation, you must learn to identify these instantly. When there are facts, legal principals, arguments, theorems, stratagems, and red herrings that confront you, you must fully understand the Socratic Method.

Is the questioner in the discourse at the beginning of this book revealing something? Is the answerer being guided? Is the entire text thesis or antithesis? Or both? Is the answerer guiding the questioner? Is the answerer the grand master of the Socratic Method? Is there an objective? If so, who gains the initiative? Who has the Advantage? Are the 5 C's at work? Who won?

If you can answer none of the questions above, you are a beginner. If you can answer these questions, but later change your perspective, you are a beginner. If you can't or can answer these questions, but can identify the thesis and antithesis and synthesis, you may be in the initial stages of becoming adept. If you see all the text conclusively, you are a master. Remember, you cannot rush enlightenment.

— See The Gorin No Sho by Myomoto Musashi.

Thesis

A thesis is a proposition to be maintained or proved. Depending on your tactic to gain the initiative (see Gorin No Sho) the thesis of any unit of litigation must be discerned. Most often 2 thesis exist or more. You must identify them all. It is wise to keep a sufficient legal dictionary and collegiate dictionary when litigating. It is wise to learn grammar. Identifying thesis in litigation is the first key to victory.

You must know the meaning of every written word in litigation, so you can identify context. In litigation, thesis lives in context.

Antithesis

The antithesis is the direct opposite or contrast. It is said that the opposite of truth is one's own perception. Perspective defines winners from losers. When you believe there is only one perspective or only a certain general perspective or a common perspective that is agreeable to all parties involved, you invite defeat. The antithesis is understood best by the perspectivist.

The antithesis of your life or profession or belief is found outside the core principle and structure of the aforementioned. The untrained are opposed to the opposition.

Truth would reveal a fear of understanding an opposed view. Victory for the opposition does not exist in understanding the views of the opposition, it is in emphatically the opposite. Defeat waits for your adversary when you understand its perspective. Defeat is certain when you understand its perspective more thoroughly than it does. This is the antithesis. Reflect on this profoundly.

Synthesis

Synthesis is the combining of elements into a whole. Socrates believed you cannot start a discourse until the antagonist agree on a single point. Synthesis in litigation is like sweetness is to sugar. Creating synthesis in litigation is an art, it takes skill, discipline, and submission to the will of THE WAY.

Synthesis is the vehicle used on the road to victory. This is synthesis.

Logic

Logic involves the study of arguments and their use in reasoning. Logic can help us to know when people hope to fool us into accepting "conclusions" based on insufficient, irrelevant, or contradictory "evidence."

Be warned, disputes and arguments in the everyday sense of these words are outside deductive reasoning and formal logic cannot resolve these matters. Logic addresses absolute certainty only. Study this well.

There are rules for our reasoning. One is identity. This principal is simple. If a statement is true, then it is true; and if it is false, then it is false. However, the truth maybe a false statement. You must study this even more.

Another rule is contradiction. This rule is simple. It states that no statement can hold true and false simultaneously. When "yes" and "no" applies to one statement, then one of these words have a double meaning. Study this always.

Another rule comes from the binary system of logic where all statements are either true or false. This rule is used in traditional logic. This is called the law of excluded middle. Where when we do not know if a statement is true or false, we assume that it must be one or the other. This assumption must be agreed on and must follow one way. Study this constantly.

A premise gives a reason to accept the conclusion. A proposition that relies on no premise is a theorem. When you join two sentences with logical implication, we call the "implying" sentence the antecedent. We call the "implied" sentence the consequent. Study this closely.

Fuzzy logic has degrees of truth, unlike binary and trinary (true false neutral), logic. Fuzzy logic has "ranges" from completely, true or false, to partially, partially neutral, totally neutral, totally true or false; these ranges can be calibrated and interchanged. Study this more closely than before.

When using logic, always search for proof. However, be aware some proof is not valid logic reasoning. The fact a thing happened on numerous occasions does not mean it happens in all instances.

Be vigilant of misuse of context, arguments of circumstance, fallacies based on a conclusion with two premises, inductive reasoning (unlike deductive reasoning, logics rigorous method of proof, inductive reasoning has no such method), paradoxes and two pronged defenses (such as "I can't be guilty of robbery because I stole counterfeit money"). Again at all times, stay vigilant of these methods.

Uncertainty Principle

The uncertainty principle was fathered by Werner Heisenberg and expanded by Schrodinger. The crux of the principle is as follows: The more precisely the position of [something] determined;

the less precisely its momentum can be known. What does this mean? Well, it is still being debated.

However, Schrodinger did an experiment with a cat. Where he placed a cat in a box then put a lid on it. At the moment the lid is placed on the box, the cat's position becomes uncertain. This is what he sought to prove.

Likewise, the law is evolutional and the more precisely the position of the law is determined; the less precisely its momentum (evolution) can be known. Constitutional rights get expanded, statutes get amended, rules get replaced by more definite rules, and procedures get interpreted and re-interpreted constantly. The law, meaning court rulings, becomes binding and non-binding in great number.

All this energy creates momentum. A litigant must know how to wield this principle of uncertainty against its adversarial object. You must understand positioning when formulating a strategy.

— See The Art of Strategy by R.L. Wang.

As you have just learned a theorem in quantum physics, you must learn the position of every continuum of legal reasoning in your respective litigating arena. I suggest you use "Schrodinger's cat." If you place a cat in a box and place a lid on it, without seeing the cat how will you know if it is breathing or alive or dead or scared or bored or sleeping ... I could go on forever. Do not fall victim to the principle of uncertainty. It will most certainly bring about defeat.

Pragmatic Reasoning

Quick correct reasoning is an art you have to learn in litigation. You must be a very attentive listener. In the book of water (see The Gorin No Sho), it's taught that you must clear your mind where you function and respond the same when there is chaos or calm.

Pragmatic reasoning is the ability to identify and use substantive elements in litigation at will. You are considered a student of pragmatic reasoning when you can listen to a muddled proposition, even an abstract contention or point of view charged at discrediting you and identify and use its substantive elements to defeat your opponent or gain an advantage or the initiative. You must employ vigilance and poise when practicing pragmatic reasoning. In litigation, you listen, read, and convey, with the sole purpose to strike first (see Gorin No Sho).

Non-Negotiable Conflict

In litigation, no negotiation exist. Most often litigated negotiations are not actually negotiations. For example, plea agreements which are usually the result of 90% of all criminal cases[19] and governed by contract law are called negotiations, but are anything but. You must be resigned before you begin any litigation process or hearing.

When you pick up the sword, you must understand it has no other purpose but to kill (see Gorin No Sho). You pick up the sword when negotiations have failed.

---

[19] Lafler v. Cooper, 132 S.Ct. 1376 (2012); Missouri v. Frye, 132 S.Ct. 1399 (2012.

The art of negotiation does not co-exist with THE ART of winning litigation. They are not even opposites. Reflect on this profoundly.

Non-negotiable conflict (see R.L. Wang Art of Strategy), is only for the trained, the disciplined, the submissive. Your reasoning has to begin with resignation. Your reason for litigating has to be desperate. The Art of Strategy by R.L. Wang conditions your mind state for the very specific purpose of THE ART of winning litigation. Do not be fooled into negotiation when litigating. Do not negotiate when you litigate. Reflect on this profoundly.

Book III

Staying:

    The Course for all pro se

    criminal litigants.

    www.anotherchance4legal.com

    It is all summed: Will we

    die for something, or die

        for nothing?

Advantage

The Genealogy of Morals by Friedrich Nietzsche will condition you to accept different hidden perspectives found within yourself. It will challenge most of your core beliefs. Litigation most often does the same. Embrace it as a friend.

No Legs

A person with no legs can't expect to sprint the fastest in a race; however, it can win every race it enters. Reflect on this profoundly.

Do not compare your absence of certain abilities, gifts, or skills against another's presence of the aforementioned. Do not follow your heart when litigating. Do not follow your adversary or your allies. Follow the will of THE ART of winning litigation.

D-Day

The cultures and lifestyles embraced by the pro se criminal litigant places it at a huge disadvantage, not to be overlooked.

Distractions permeate these lifestyles and cultures usually as a result of disfunctionalism and lack of identity. Coupled with other obstacles cited supra, the only hope for a victory for a pro se criminal litigation is to submit to the will of THE ART of winning litigation. There is no other hope. Religion also factors as well. However, THE ART of winning litigation can co-exist with any religious practice.

Winning

My first victory using this transmission was won when I didn't understand how the courts worked. I studied and passed the "staying" course and sent a guy home from prison as a result. He was sentenced to over a decade. I sent the initial habeas corpus petition to the appellate court, which was an error. The appellate court corrected this error with no penalty. I didn't believe I would or wouldn't be victorious. However, I was resigned to the task. I submitted to the will of THE ART of winning litigation.

I was ultimately victorious. The Assistant United States Attorney I defeated was a heralded grandmaster. So how did I win with such little knowledge? When I didn't understand where to send the petition?

Grants of Advantage

Often pro se criminal litigators believe they have to use methods they truly don't understand. Winning litigation is Triple AAA: aggressive, assertive, and availing. There is case law[20]which provides all pro se litigants with Supreme Advantage. Relaying **your** point **accurately, briefly** and **clearly (abc)** promotes, bolsters, emboldens, and advocates victory. However, elegance, reciting confounding proposition and theory, flaunting and flouting court rules and prior decisions, promote, advocate, and ensure defeat. If you start off in an elevated position, end in an elevated position. Always use the advantage.

The Way of Argument

If you and a priest were assisting your grandmother to the hospital while you were being

---

[20] Haines v. Kerner. 404 U.S. 519, 520 (1972) (per curiam); Castro v. United States, 540 U.S. 375, 383 (2003).

accused of having an affair, the first thing you would do is get the priest and your grandmother to vouch for you. You would not argue the elements of the accusation. Therefore, your argument must be independent, brief, clear, and accurate. This is the way of THE ART of winning litigation. You must reflect on this profoundly.

Kotteakos V. United States, 328 U.S. 750 (1946)

Error permeates everything man does and does constantly. No trial or legal proceeding is without error. Read *Kotteakos*, it will explain as much. Whatever binds you in your litigation, be assured there is always a linchpin that when removed, unbounds you.

The "staying" course ensures you will be able to locate and remove this linchpin. Be aware sometimes several linchpins appear to exist. However, do not be led astray, there is only one in each case. You must be trained not to become attached to or intrigued with fallacy or speciousness. Train hard.

Without Mastery

When you become adept in the "staying" course, you will find the confidence to stand and converse with those further trained and practiced. Correct those who believe they are superior in intellect and knowledge. Without mastery, you will be recognized as grounded and well versed in the fundamentals of criminal law. You will not be able to be fooled or tricked or persuaded. Never belie your training.[21]

---

[21]

Book IV

A Wo/Man's Life:

> To figure from failures
>
> how not to fail is to figure
>
> how to be successful.

Advantage

L ' Politics by Aristotle should bring your character into question. You cannot know your characteristics if you have not examined your character. You cannot win a war without knowing your enemies' characteristics. You cannot utilize your enemies' characteristics until you know your own. If your enemy knows your characteristics and you do not, not only will you lose, you will be destroyed.

In Your Hands

Detachment is a defensive and protective psychological tactic used by us all. Willingly or unwillingly, knowingly or unknowingly, you must detach to litigate. To be overtly subjective is to be primed for failure in litigation.

THE ART of winning litigation teaches detachment to beget submission to the will of THE ART of winning litigation. This is THE WAY (see Art of Strategy).

Criminal law usually holds in its balance the life or liberty or property of something. Most often, it's your life or liberty you are defending or someone else. Regardless of the subject of the life or liberty whether it is yours or someone else, getting personally involved ensures corruption. Do not become corrupt in practicing THE ART of winning litigation. As you will no longer follow the will of THE ART of winning litigation, but a perversed rendition of the former.

Corruption

If you are prosperous, but lose significantly more than you win in your litigations, you are corrupt. If you don't care about victory and only a fair result, you are corrupt. If you believe justice is a tool of law enforcement, you are corrupt. If you render the law ambiguous for power or favor, you are corrupt. If you litigate to prove you are right, you are corrupt. If you litigate for reprisal, you are corrupt. If you litigate with rapacious intent, you are corrupt. If you are corrupt, you do not follow the will of THE ART of winning litigation.

If you perfectly align a thing to go from one point to the next, it is not corrupt. So is THE WAY of THE ART of winning litigation. However, the slightest variation or alteration in alignment will prove, the longer you travel, to be off course, out of line, corrupted; it will not reach the prespecified destination. This is corruption.

You must remember-the prospect of life and liberty and property are in your hands always. You are its custodian, its guardian, it is often brought to you in very unsavory and dislikeable garb, or it may come in seductive packaging. However it comes, do not induce corruption, follow corruption, or continue to follow your own corruption. Great civilizations have fallen disregarding this warning. Reflect on this profoundly.

THE ART Is Justice

In the perception of THE ART of winning litigation, we are all equal.

Justice will choose the balance THE ART itself will choose the victor. THE ART of winning litigation is a system within the ecosystem of justice. They co- exist harmoniously. As justice is harmonious, thereto is THE ART of winning litigation. Justice cannot be wielded.

Because we are all equal, we all have the opportunity of victory. THE ART of winning litigation trains us to identify and seize this opportunity before our opponent. Justice will choose the balance. Do not concern yourself with justice. If you follow THE ART of winning litigation, you do not follow corruption. Therefore, thoughts of offending justice are distractions. THE ART is justice.

How Much Does a Commander Charge

I had a client once that hounded me about his indictment. He was persistent. I found an error, via the "staying" course, in his case. It would bring him relief. However, he persisted about his indictment. After refocusing, I found it wasn't his indictment per se, but it did involve his indictment.

He had a speedy trial issue which he won in a prior hearing. However, he was superseded. Speedy trial is an affirmative defense[22] without appeal the government could not supersede pursuant to the case law in his district.

He was right and I failed him. Although he knew no law, he submitted to THE WAY of winning litigation. I was victorious, he was released. However, I had left the path of victory for the

---

[22] United States v. Ferreira, 665 F.3d 701 (6th Cir. 2011).

path of granting some relief. He paid me handsomely.

Another client I had was represented by a professor at a prominent university in Washington, D.C. I found the error in his case which he passed on to the professor. The professor very reluctantly adopted it. He was granted release because of the error I found. The professor took credit for the victory.[23] The professor made 50 times more money than I did for this case.

Finally, I had a client who I helped pro bono. He had filed several attacks at his multi-decade sentence, to no avail. He had filed challenging the execution of his sentence within the institution he was held[24] before he sought my assistance. I found he was actually innocent of his crime.[25] He was subsequently released from federal custody. We were victorious because we both followed the will of THE ART of winning litigation.

How much should a commander charge his country for winning a war? Do not be mistaken, THE ART of winning litigation does not only yield to commanders, you must gain your own understanding and enlightenment from all of the above. It may mean a wo/man's life.

Know It All

The only way to find the error / issue or present the offense or defense that will garner you victory is to know the facts, the fundamentals, the rules, the procedures, and the stare decisis of the arena. Know it all. When they all align, victory is the next point.

---

[23] Brooks v. United States, 39 A.3d 873 (D.C 2002).
[24] In re Dorsainvil, 119 F.3d 245, 251 (3rd Cir. 1997).
[25] Whiteside v. United States, 748 F.3d 541 (4th Cir. 2014); Herrera v. Collins, 506 U.S. 309 (1993).

a. Bias

Read without bias or predisposition. Listen without bias by listening without fear of being proven incorrect. If I am bias, I can be easily moved about the courtroom as a warrior who is intended on not relinquishing a certain position. S/he leaves itself vulnerable to being pinned, surrounded, or flanked. Reflect on this profoundly.

b. Clear Thought

Do not be preoccupied when trying a case or litigating. The most complex propositions are built on simplicity. Opposing views, conflict and uncertainty, are prerequisites of confusion. Keep your mind clear by being thoroughly prepared. You do this by identifying weapons and tactics. As with a warrior, few adversaries master an exhaustive number of techniques, tactics, and weapons. If you know beforehand what each weapon, tactic, and technique are used for, once you identify your adversaries, confusion is obsolete. If you're not thinking as clear as you like, or become perplexed in a legal contest, you haven't prepared properly.

c. Fundamentals

The more fundamentally balanced combatant wins. Michael Phelps won his record breaking gold metal by a fraction of a second because, as he acknowledged, the guy in the lead raised his head a second too early when reaching for the wall at the finish.

Had he stayed fundamentally balanced, he would have won, but he raised his head and he lost. If you ever decide that being fundamental in an instance will delay time or is otherwise unnecessary, know you have decided to welcome and embrace defeat. Reflect on this profoundly.

d. Nothing Easy

Don't expect anything to be easy. A trial where someone is caught on camera in broad daylight with a million witnesses, is most often less difficult than more obscure cases. Nothing in litigation is easy. Underestimating the difficulty of the proceeding or task is ensuring defeat.

e. Objective Cognition

To find the winning issue, you must know the XYZ of winning litigation. The XYZ of THE ART of winning litigation is eXamine, know the whY, and Zero in on the resolution.

Full contextual assessment is how you eXamine: (1) Inquire into the nature or condition of the legal situation; (2) Look closely at the things you eXamine; and (3) Then test them by questioning it yourself and anything relevant. This is the X of the XYZ of winning litigation.

Know the whY. WhY will this matter? (1) Is it key and material; (2) Will it undermine something significantly material; (3) Is it cumulative? If so it is not significant; and (4) What else undermines what you have examined? If there is a thing that does, then know what you examined does not matter. This is the Y of the XYZ of winning litigation.

Finally, once you know why this matters legally, you then Zero in on the thing you have examined and found why it undermines the entire matter in question.

When you Zero in: (1) Find what emboldens this one specific thing and never rely on what's merely cumulative to do this; (2) Once you have correctly embolden this one specific thing, make it legally more credible, plausible, and significant, then what it undermined; and (3) Present it as if it should have always been evident without flaunting or flouting. This, is the Z of the XYZ of winning litigation.

This is how you find / argue / present a winning error / issue/ claim in any legal matter or arena. You must master the XYZ.

Book V

A

B

C

You can do anything you put

your full mind to if you are

willing to give up the belief

that you can't.

Advantage

The Art of Effective Communication by Rakesh N. Praqya, this book is self-explanatory. In litigation, we have to make the opponent want to communicate with us and further believe in your point. Also read Immediate Fiction by Jerry Cleaver, it will also help you in achieving this.

Accuracy

The quickest way to be seen as incredulous in the opinion of the court, your opponents, and if you have allies, is to employ inaccuracy. If this occurs, you are no longer relevant in the contest. You have to necessitate accuracy. Accuracy should not be confused with correctness as it is an element of correctness, not correctness itself. Always be accurate.

Brief

The grandmaster of this transmission employed a deadly tool known to all his students as "the black pen." When wielded by the grandmaster, this "black pen" would turn a 3 page motion into a paragraph and a half.

I was taught you have 2 ears and 1 mouth for a reason. Listen twice as much as you speak. Being overly verbose bornes incredulity.

Being brief is so detrimental to communicating your point that Barack Obama in his first campaign for president changed the verbose style he used for years to convey his message. At the time he made this decision, he was considered among Americans, a master of rhetoric, a champion of muddled conjecture, a lecturer of lofty propositions, and ultimately an elites out of touch with Americans.

If Barack Obama who is a legendary all- time great grandmaster of effective and persuasive communications; steadfastly employs being brief, you should take being brief seriously. If you don't, you encourage your demise.

Clear

Easily seen or heard; evident. This is the definition of clear. When understanding clarity, think of Shakespeare. His writings have an opaque literariness when juxtaposed against today's writings. However, what is most clear is a point he wanted to get across. To be or not to be that is the question. In the book 'immediate fiction ' (which I strongly suggest to any trial attorney and litigant claiming actual innocence), the author shows you an unedited version of Shakespeare's "To Be or Not To Be." It is very lengthy.

Another popular quote is from the litigative realm. "If the glove don't fit, you must acquit. "It was used for clarity. A very complicated, emotionally perplexing and highly publicized case. Where the winning attorneys cut down chaos and confusion with clarity. The statement was materially accurate, brief and clear and obviously their opponents did not grasp the seriousness and importance of this, many still do not today.

Fail to make someone who is uninterested understand your position, the counter position, your proposal and why you should win, in less than 1 minute; then you do not embrace clarity and you do not understand how to employ it. Reflect on this profoundly.

"[Write]-A-Way"

All effective litigation is persuasive. You have to illicit and induce the response you want. Always use as many paragraphs to get an idea across, but make each paragraph less than 12 lines ("pre-teen"). Moreover, write so you do not need to italicize, capitalize, or emphasize. Finally, stay away from legalese (especially when pro se). Legalese are Latin or French terms that can be substituted for other words or phrases.

Example

Keep your subject and verb close:

#1 I ran but was beaten by the assailant.

[unclear and muddled — wrong]

#2 The assailant beat me as I ran.

[clear and less words — right]

Unless you want to emphasize the object rather than the subject in a sentence, write assertively, not passively.

Book VI

Fact

From

Fiction

Creating Separation:

Those who are aware of triumph

when it is obvious also to others

do not have excellent skills.

Those who triumph during conflict

while the world says, "well done!"

do not have excellent skills.

Book VI

Advantage

The Art of Love by OVID is the book I suggest for Book VI. If you don't know what love is, there is no way to properly love yourself which means you cannot properly love what you do. You must love to submit to the will of THE ART of winning litigation.

Fiction

Fiction can be disputed, a fact cannot. Fiction is driven by personal perception, opinion and conclusion. Although law can be made in this way, winning litigation cannot. Moreover, the Constitution is anything but personal. Fiction appeals and belies disbelief. Winning litigation persuades and belies error. You must know these are not the same.

Fact

Law often changes, facts do not. A fact in litigation is like ammunition and artillery in war. The only facts that matter in THE ART of winning litigation are those that are material and conceded to by both sides. Undisputed facts are the deadliest. However, you must be careful in a trial setting with a jury because they decide these facts. Favorable proven facts or favorable facts not disproved are "death blow" facts in THE ART of winning litigation. However, they must be significantly material and you must be careful not to be fooled. Study this well.

Factual Statement

Speaking or writing anything, while litigating, that is not fact is like covering your ears to

Book VI

hear. In THE ART of winning litigation, we do not muddle the advancement of our position by stating or relying on personal opinion or assumption. Law is applied to facts. This is evident when you begin to read case law. Facts determine victory. Therefore, facts are more powerful than law in THE ART of winning litigation.

Do You Believe

The hot coffee argument where McDonalds was sued seems silly until you know the facts. Then it becomes very serious. The right to confront your accuser is a law;[26] however, pursuant to case law, many different facts are applied to this law. In litigation, your configuration of facts must be believable. Even litigations won by technicality are believable. Your believability influences your victory.

Fact Mastery

Shun opinion, novelty, what's appealing, and work from only the relevant material facts first. This is fact mastery. This is the method to separating fact from fiction. Reflect on this profoundly. There is nothing else to reveal on this subject.

---

[26] Crawford v. Washington, 541 U.S. 36 (2004); United States v. Jackson, 625 F.3d 875 (5th Cir. 2010); United States v. Ignasiak, 667 F.3d 1217, 1231 (11th Cir. 2012).

Book VII

The

Arena:

Always take an indirect route.
Lure your opponent by holding out
advantages. Start out after them,
and arrive before them.

Advantage

Letter from a Birmingham prison by Martin Luther King Jr. A perfect example of the mentality, focus, and will needed to win. When there is no hope, THE ART of winning litigation prevails, always.

How to Win

Winning is a state of being. THE ART of winning litigation is fundamental balance. You must have superior fundamental balance to win. If your opponent is powerful, but fundamentally unbalanced, you will win using THE ART of winning litigation. This is your method.

Fundamental Balance

To fear the misapplication or non-application of the fundamentals is the beginning to achieving fundamental balance. For criminal law, these fundamentals are found in the "staying" course. In other areas of litigation, the same principles apply.

You must continuously practice and adhere to the fundamentals to achieve balance. Balance is being adept in all things fundamental.

Tactic

Strategy is the overarching plan. Tactics are what is needed to effect this strategy. The Gorin No Sho is the best in teaching tactics. R.L. Wang's the Art of Strategy is the best in teaching strategy. THE ART of winning litigation is the best in teaching winning litigation. A master tactician would never overlook this fact.

You must know how to strike without actually striking overtly. You must know **Ken No Sen,** **Tai No Sen, Tai Tai No Sen,** the rules to striking first. You must know this, thoroughly.

Ippon Michi

The way of the first strike is the rule of one strike one kill and the cornerstone of THE ART of winning litigation. This takes attentive poise. You must always be poised to strike to kill. Every opponent that does not follow THE ART of winning litigation will allow for you to implement 'one strike one kill' during a contest. Be vigilant. However, if you can't identify this brief window of opportunity, you have chosen to pass up victory. Fundamental balance is the only way to engender Ippon Michi.

Outside of Litigation

There are many domains you must study outside of litigation to make you a master of winning litigation. Theatre, philosophy, speech writing, public speaking, grammar, debating, psychology, interrogation tactics, and communication without speech ... the list is non-exhaustive. Follow your intuition in this regard. Enlightenment is found within. Nothing is frivolous if it enhances your practice in litigation. Reflect on this profoundly.

Belief

Do not believe in yourself, believe in your ability to follow THE ART of winning litigation. It will lead you to victory.

Therefore, you will not make the error of trying to employ self-confidence, as confidence is a state of being and cannot be employed. Confidence is exuded when your belief in your ability to perfectly or effectively execute a system is unshakable. Put your belief in your ability. Reflect on this profoundly.

No Fear

Fear exist to convince you not to find out, what if. In THE ART of winning litigation, fear cannot exist as THE ART it-self convinces you of nothing but victory. This is why we submit to it and choose not to submit to fear. You can only serve one master. You can only submit to one thing.

Objective

Objectives are made when strategizing; victory is the only objective in winning litigation. However, escaping the inevitable is to defeat your opponent. If the inevitable assures that I lose my kingdom and all my army at the end of a contest, victory would lie in losing half my army and half my kingdom at the end of a contest. Be cautioned, you do not choose where victory lies in THE ART of winning litigation. THE ART will choose. You must merely submit. This is your objective. You must reflect on this carefully.

Situation

The Art of Strategy by R.L. Wang shows you how to identify situations. There are 9 such situations. If you don't know your situation, you will lose. There are different strategies for different situations. You must know them all. Most litigants don't identify their situation until it is over. Seize what is held dearest and everyone else will comply, conform, and concur. However, you will find it perplexing and impossible to seize anything if you don't understand the situation.

Distinguishing Defeat

Most winnable contests are not pursued inter alia because of "Uncle Moe," momentum. Grandmasters are immune to the opposition's momentum. It is only to be factored when it rallies your opponent as your spirit must remain at all times greater. Most momentum rallies and emboldens the spirit. However, to allow opposing momentum to convince you to surrender is evidence you lack the ability to distinguish defeat.

Myomoto Musashi believed you must employ the long and short sword in a contest (see Gorin No Sho). Learning this style is more difficult. However, it allows you to be ready for every situation. If your opponent attacks with a long sword outside, you drive them inside as the long sword is less effective inside (see Gorin No Sho).

It may take considerable time to do this. During this course you may seem to be losing the contest or have lost the contest. However, once you drive (by any means) your opponent inside, you have the advantage over the long sword; if you have a short sword. This is to distinguish defeat. Reflection is needed.

When distinguishing defeat, you must be objective. Law is fluid.

This is the reason for laws (statutes) that limit your ability to use favorable changes in law.[27] These are merely obstacles and you must be objective in your assessment of them given your situation. Defeat exist where, per your knowledge, there aren't any viable options left. Victory lies in every viable option. However, these options may not exist because you do not know them. THE ART of winning litigation teaches that even when your strategy fails, your opponent may not have achieved victory.

Victory is finality in victory. Winning is not absolute as you can be winning and then fall to defeat. Victory can never fall to defeat. This is how you distinguish defeat. Reflect on this profoundly.

Know Your Weakness

The mirror can be a deadly foe. Know your weakness. List them all. List everything you want to improve about your issue, theory, argument, claim or ability to litigate effectively. Ask others, because if you are not willing to acknowledge your weakness, in the arena to a master, this will become evident at first glance. Before the contest begins, you will have relinquished the advantage and given away the initiative and embraced defeat.

I often hear "I've done this 1,000 times" or "I know my argument/issue." However, this may or may not be true. Inconsequently, it is only a minuscule portion of the beginning. If all you know is parts of the beginning, then you concede you will not recognize the end.

If victory is the end as THE ART of winning litigation teaches, you will never recognize victory. Know your weakness and your opponent's weakness will be manifestly identifiable.

---

[27] Phelps V. Alameida, 569 F.3d 1120 (9th Cir. 2007); Agostini v. Felton, 521 U.S. 203, 239 (1997).

Chasing the Truth

Litigation is not about the truth, it is about proving a theory. It must give the appearance of justice[28] (not harmony) and ring true. You must know this well. It must also include the best interest of the public.[29] This is litigation.

The truth cares not who it hurts or helps; therefore, litigation is not the truth. Do not chase it. THE ART of winning litigation is only concerned about victory, obtainable through winning litigation — not victory obtain able through winning truth. You must be wise in this decision. Do not chase the truth when litigating.

Licensed To Kill

You must have the will to kill (meaning defeat) anyone who steps in the litigation arena against you. Do not concern yourself with collateral matters or anything ancillary. Meaning specifically (the 4 R's): repercussion, retribution, revenge, or reputation. Do not file, communicate, or advance anything in litigation that, within the rules, does not directly bring about the demise of your opponent. However, you should have calculated all the collateral factors when forming your strategy (see R.L. Wang's Art of Strategy). Study this carefully.

P' Aggression

Be more aggressive at the end of a litigation and be very aggressive at the beginning of a litigation.

---

[28] In re Murchison, 349 U.S. 133, 136 (1955).
[29] United States v. Foster, 507 F.3d 233, 249-52 (4th Cir. 2007).

THE ART of winning litigation teaches P₃'Aggression: Passively aggressive, palpably aggressive, and plainly aggressive. You must be adept in employing them. Knowing your situation is key to P_3 Aggression, as you can be tricked into defeat. You must gain your own enlightenment of each word. Reflect on this profoundly.

The Jones'

In <u>Jones</u>, 463 U.S. 745 (1983), the Supreme Court warned against excessive litigation.[30] Do not get the Jones' when litigating. Alternative or multiple theories or claims can only be useful as a tactic, if ever useful, and only in the possession of a grandmaster. Never use this as a strategy. It is error and easily defeatable.

W.H.A.T. I s the True Adversary

Know your true adversary. When wielding a knife against a machine gun, or multiple machine guns, your true adversary is what? The numbers? The machine gunist? The machine gun? Red herrings and semantics are often employed in litigation to keep hidden the true adversary.

<u>W</u>

---

[30] McCleskey v. Zant, 494 U.S. 467, 494 (1991); Sanders v.United States, 373 U.S. 1, 18 (1963).

The true adversary in the illustration above is superior weaponry. The weaponry is so superior it supersedes skill and garners the advantage. This is the **W**hat.

Book VII

H

How do you overcome this superior weaponry? Of course, by gaining the initiative. You must be practiced in doing this. I will leave this to your own enlightenment. This is the **H**ow.

A

When you know how to gain the initiative, you attack. Know all the ways of attack. There is always more than one. Write them down if you have to. This is the **A**ttack.

T

Every contest has a rhythm, its own timing. You must know this timing intimately (see Gorin No Sho). You must practice this timing. In wielding a knife against multiple machine gunners, or even one, timing is crucial. The time for 'one strike one kill' is fleeting. THE ART of winning litigation dictates you must seize this superior weaponry for this is what is held dearest to your opponent. You must be on time. This is the **T**iming.

In the example above, there are several ways per the illustration to obtain victory against the machine gunners. Think of your own ways. Test them thoroughly. Get someone to strategize against you using the scenario. If you don't believe there is, or have not figured out a way to victory per the illustration above, you are not ready to submit to the will of THE ART of winning litigation. This is so.

Victory

For those who follow THE ART of winning litigation, you will find victory. Victory through submission, this submission will ensure you will make no error. If you make no error in your strategy, in your tactic, in following THE ART of winning litigation, you will find victory and you will find defeat for your enemy.

THE ART of winning litigation teaches you to identify, advance, and obtain victory. When you become skilled at this, you will create a situation that cannot be defeated and will miss no opportunity at defeating your opponent.

Through this transmission, I discharge my duty as obligated per THE WAY of THE GREAT ART.

Index to Appendix

A2 Constitutional Rights

(Generally Effected)

- The U.S. Constitution has been doctrine since 1803 -

The Fourth Amendment protects an individual's personal rights: unreasonable search and seizure, issues of restraint and intrusions by state or government and issues surrounding your detainment or when you are being interrogated. A case called United States v. White, 322 U.S. 694 (1944), speaks of this Amendment. Also, Supreme Court cases like Miranda, Wong Sun, Mapp, Terry v. Ohio, and Stone v. Powell, are popular.

The Fifth Amendment protects against issues of indictment, double jeopardy, self-incrimination, Due process, equal protections and private property taken for public use.

The Sixth Amendment protects speedy and public trial rights, trial by impartial jury, right to trial in state and district in which crime is committed, right to be informed of nature and cause of accusation, right to confront witnesses, right to compulsory process for obtaining witnesses, and right to the assistance of counsel for defense.

The Seventh Amendment applies to all civil rights sanctions for damages and entitles one to a jury trial. However, if a lawsuit for equity (injunction) is advanced, the protections of the Seventh Amendment do not apply.

The Eight Amendment protects that right against excessive bail and fines, and the right against cruel and unusual punishment.

The Fourteenth Amendment also has its own state Due Process protections for state laws. See Missouri P.R. Co. v. Humes, 115 U.S 512 (1885); Dreyer v. Illinois, 187 U.S 71 (1902) and Herbert v. Louisiana, 272 U.S/ 312 (1926); and also has its own equal protections right of state laws. See Perley v. North Carolina, 249 U.S. 510 (1919).

A3   7 Structural Errors

7 STRUCTURAL ERRORS

Structural errors are "fundamental constitutional errors" that defy the analysis by "harmless error" standards. See Arizona v. Fulminate, 499 U.S. 279 (1991).

1. Gideon v. Wainwright, 372 U.S. 335 (1963) (total deprivation of the right counsel).
2. Tumey v. Ohio, 273 U.S. 510 (1927) (lack of an impartial trial judge).
3. Vasquez v. Hillary 474 U.S. 254 (1986) (unlawful exclusion of grand jurors of defendant's race).
4. McKaskle v. Wiggins, 465 U.S. 168 (1984) (the right to self-representation at trial).
5. Waller v. Georgia, 467 U.S. 39 (1984) (right to a public trial).
6. Sullivan v. Louisiana 508 U.S. 275 (1993) (erroneous reasonable-doubt instruction to jury).
7. Gonzales v. Lopez, 548 U.S. 140, (2006) (deprivation of the right counsel of choice).

A4   The 45 Rights We Should All Know

THE 45 RIGHTS WE SHOULD ALL KNOW

"Prevention and incapacitation are often legitimate goals. Some classes of criminals commit scores of offenses before they are caught, so one conviction may reflect years of criminal activity. There are realistic limits to efforts at rehabilitation. We must try, however, to bridge the gap between proper skepticism about rehabilitation on the one hand and improper refusal to acknowledge that the more than two million inmates in the United States are human beings."

-Justice Kennedy

"Retribution is completely distinct from community outrage. Retribution is not lex talionis "an eye for an eye"".

-Gerard V. Bradley

1. The Fourth Amendment to the United States Constitution guarantees the right to be free from unreasonable searches and seizures.
2. This extends to individuals, houses, vehicles, papers, computers, electronic devices, etc.
3. The protection of the Fourth Amendment governs arrests, searches and seizures, unconstitutional invasions personal privacy and liberty, stop and frisks, arrest and search warrants, electronic surveillance, and other protected areas.
4. "Probable cause" is a critical concept of the Fourth Amendment and is required in order for any arrests, warrants, and other governmental intrusions to be constitutionally reasonable.
5. What is "probable cause?" "Probable cause" is a reasonable ground for suspicion, supported by circumstances that a crime has been committed or is being committed.

6. What is a "search?" A "search" is defined as "something more than a superficial, external examination. It entails 'looking through.' 'rummaging,' 'probing,' 'scrutiny,' and 'examining internally.' "United States v. Snow, 44 F. 3d 133, 135 (2nd Cir. 1995).
7. What is a "seizure?" A "seizure" has multiple meanings, one relating top property and different on for the seizure of a person. A seizure as it relates to property is the taking hold of possession of an individual's property. A seizure of a person occurs when the person is not free to leave.
8. All arrest and search warrants may only be issued if supported by probable cause.

9. All arrests are require probable cause. Probable cause arrest exists when the police have knowledge or reliable information of facts and circumstances that crime has been or is being committed.
10. Once under arrest, a suspect automatically is subjected to a search and this includes all bags and containers that a suspect is carrying. This search may be conducted without a warrant.
11. For arrests and searches both with and without a warrant to be lawful, probable cause is required.
12. The Fourth Amendment shields an individual against intrusions that violate a reasonable expectation of privacy, i.e., an overnight guest in a residence and standing to challenge unlawful entries and searches of the home.
13. If incriminating evidence is discovered in plain view or visible to an officer, its seizure is justified.
14. Electronic surveillance such as wire-tapping, eaves dropping, monitoring communications, and computer usage are subject to the protections of the Fourth Amendment.
15. Officer's attachment of GPS tracking device to vehicle and subsequent use of that device to monitor vehicle's movements was an unconstitutional invasion of privacy. United States v. Jones, 132 S.Ct. 945,949 (2012).
16. A search incident that leads to an arrest doesn't allow a routine search of the arrestees' mobile phones. See Riley v. California, 2014 BL 175779, 95 CRL 445 (U.S. 2014).
17. Without reasonable, articulable suspicion, the police cannot justify a stop, detention, and pat down of an individual; and any evidence obtained as a result of this illegal search and seizure, is inadmissible in the court of law.
18. Under certain circumstances, a warrantless nonconsensual search of an automobile is justified. These situations include; when a driver is stopped for violating a traffic offense, border searches, etc.
19. Police-citizen interactions which take place under circumstances which an individual's 'freedom to walk away' is terminated and briefly detained is termed a Terry stop. See Terry v. Ohio, 392 U.S. 1 (1968). You have the freedom to walk away if police cannot articulate what crime you committed.
20. After a traffic stop and officer returns the driver's license and registration, the driver is free to leave and any consent to search automobile is voluntary.

21. The police can detain an eyewitness to a crime if exigent circumstances exist.
22. All occupants of an automobile have standing to challenge a stop, but passenger cannot challenge the search of the automobile unless s/he has a reasonable expectation of privacy in the area searched.
23. When police stop an automobile for a traffic violation, it does not give the officer justification to frisk the driver or the passengers.
24. A tip that an individual is carrying a gun, without more, cannot justify and frisk.

25. Once arrested, an officer may only ask a limited series of questions to obtain the person's name, address, and an explanation concerning their presence and conduct.
26. Stopping and individual in a high crime area/neighborhood is insufficient to justify a stop.
27. Refusing to listen, answer, or cooperate with the police does not provide justification for an investigatory stop. It is your right not to answer any questions.
28. When an arrest or search warrant is being executed, officers have a right to make a protective sweep to ensure their safety and protect themselves from the presence of danger.
29. An arrest in front of a house or near an automobile does not justify search of the house or automobile.
30. An arrest within a particular room of a house does not extend to all closed or concealed areas of the room.
31. Before an interrogation of a suspect, the police are required to advise the suspect of their Miranda rights.
32. An individual who voluntarily comes to a police station for questioning is not, without more, in custody. See Oregon v. Mathiason, 492, U.S 492, 495 (1977).
33. Even when an arrest is legally justified, excessive force during an arrest may amount to a Fourth Amendment violation.
34. Body intrusions are subject to the protections of the Fourth Amendment: e.g., the police cannot take a suspect to the hospital in order to extract evidence.
35. Articulable facts supporting a reasonable suspicion that a person suspected of a serious crime justifies a stop to question the person or to detain the person briefly while attempting to obtain further information. The Supreme Court has held that individualized suspicion is unnecessary when a vehicle is stopped briefly for questioning or observation at a sobriety or immigration checkpoint.
36. A landlord may not give consent to search a tenant's premises.
37. An individual's right to keep and bear arms for self-defense in one's home is conferred by the Second Amendment. See District of Columbia v. Heller, 554 U.S. 570, 628-30 (2008).
38. Forcing an individual to act in disregard for his/her religious beliefs, traditions, or practices violates the free exercise clause of the First Amendment. See O'Lone v. Estate of Shabazz, 482 U.S. 342, 349-53 (1987).
39. The Establishment Clause prohibits the government and its official from showing a preference for any religious denomination over another. See Larson v. Valente, 456 U.S. 228, 244 (1982).
40. The disclosure of an individual's medical records without his/her consent constitutes an invasion of personal privacy. See Whalen v. Roe, 429 U.S. 589, 598-600, 605-06 (1977); Nixon v. Administrator of General Services, 433 U.S. 425, 457-58 (1977).
41. Where an officer observes a two-way transaction between two individuals, probable cause does not exist. See Shelton v. United States, 929 A.2d 420, 424 (D.C. 2007).

42. An individual's Miranda right to remain silent is different and separate from an individual's Miranda right to have an attorney present.
43. Personal jurisdiction can be found where libelous article written by a defendant in one state causes an intentional tortious injury to the plaintiff in a different state. See Calder v. Jones, 465 U.S. 783 (1984).
44. A landlord owes his tenant or anyone on the premises with consent "ordinary care" in maintenance. If a person is lawfully on the premises and is injured due to the landlord's negligence, they are entitle to recovery.

45. In marital disputes concerning property an adverse possession must be found to be: (1) open, (2) notorious, (3) hostile (to the defendant's interest), (4) under claim of right (denying anyone else's' right), (5) exclusive, and (6) continuous.

-by Kevone Newsome

A5   Court Reporters

COURT REPORTERS

Atlantic (A.)   North Eastern (N.E):
Connecticut	New Jersey	Illinois	New York
Delaware	Pennsylvania	Indiana	Ohio
Maine	Rhode Island	Massachusetts	
Maryland	Vermont	New Hampshire	

District of Columbia (Municipal Court of Appeals)
Southern (So.):
Alabama	Florida	Louisiana	Mississippi

Superior Court, Appellate Department

West's California Reporter (Cal.):
California Supreme Court   District Courts of Appeal
Pacific P:
Alaska	Montana	Arizona	Nevada
California	New Mexico	(Sup. Ct. only)	Oklahoma
Colorado	Oregon	Hawaii	Utah South
Idaho	Washington	Kansas	Wyoming
Missouri			

South Eastern (S.E.):
Georgia	Virginia	North Carolina	West Virginia
South Carolina			

Western (W.E.):
Arkansas	Tennessee	Kentucky	Texas

New York Supplement (N.Y.S.)
Court of Appeals   Appellate Division
Miscellaneous

North Western (N.W.)
Iowa	Nebraska	Wisconsin	Michigan
North Dakota	South Dakota	Minnesota	

Federal Supplement (F. Supp.):
U.S Districts Courts   U.S. Custom Courts

Federal Rules Decisions (F.R.D.):
U.S District Courts

Federal Appendix (Fed. Appx.):
U.S. District Courts

Federal (F.):
U.S. Court of Appeals   Federal Court of Appeals

U.S Supreme Court (S.Ct.):
The Supreme Court of the United States

A6   Federal Court Addresses

FEDERAL COURT ADRESSES

United States Supreme Court
1 First Street, N.E.
Washington, D.C. 20543

United States Courts of Appeals:

District of Columbia Circuit
E. Barrett Prettyrann United States Courthouse
333 Constitution Avenue, N.W.
Room 5523
Washington, D.C. 20001

First Circuit
John Joseph Moakley United States Courthouse
One Courthouse Way, Suite 2500
Boston, MA 02210-3002

Second Circuit
Thurgood Marshall United States Courthouse
40 Centre Street, 18th Floor
New York, NY 10007-1501

Third Circuit
James A. Byrne United States Courthouse
601 Market Street, Room 21400
Philadelphia, PA 19106-1729

Fourth Circuit
Lewis F. Powell, Jr. United States Courthouse Annex
1100 East Main Street, Suite 501
Richmond, VA 23219-3525

Fifth Circuit
F. Edward Herbert Federal Building (Main Office)
600 South Maestri Place
New Orleans, LA 70130

Sixth Circuit
Potter Stewart United States Courthouse
100 East Fifth Street, Suite 540
Cincinnati, OH 45202

Seventh Circuit
Everett McKinley Dirksen United States Courthouse
219 South Dearborn Street, Room 2722
Chicago, XL 60604

Eight Circuit
Warren E. Burger Federal Building
316 North Robert Street, Room 500
St. Paul, MN 55101

Eight Circuit
Thomas F. Eagleton United States Courthouse
111 South Tenth Street, Room 24.239
St. Louis, MO 63102-1116

Ninth Circuit
Richard H. Chambers Courthouse
125 South Grand Avenue, 1st Floor
Pasadena, CA 91105-1621

Ninth Circuit
James R. Browning United States Courthouse
95 Seventh Street
San Francisco, CA 94103-1518

Ninth Circuit
The Pioneer Courthouse
700 S.W. Sixth Avenue, 1st Floor
Portland, OR 97204

Ninth Circuit
William K. Nakamura United States Courthouse
1010 Fifth Avenue, Room 430
Seattle, WA 98104-1195

Tenth Circuit
Byron White United States Courthouse
1823 Stout Street, 1st Floor
Denver, CO 80257-1823

Eleventh Circuit
Elbert P. Tuttle Court of Appeals Building
56 Forsyth Street, N.W.
Atlanta, GA 30303

United Stated District Courts:

District of Columbia Circuit
E. Barrett Prettyman United States Courthouse
333 Constitution Avenue, N.W.
Room 1225
Washington, D.C. 20001

First Circuit:

Maine:

Margaret Chase Smith Federal Building
202 Harlow Street
Bangor, ME 04401-4901

Edward T. Gignoux Federal Courthouse
156 Federal Street
Portland, ME 04101-4152

Massachusetts:

John Joseph Moakley United States Courthouse
One Courthouse Way, Suite 2300
Boston, MA 02210-300

300 State Street, Room 1-120
Springfield, MA 01105

Harold D. Donohue Federal Building and United States Courthouse
595 Main Street
Worcester, MA 01608-2025

New Hampshire:

Warren B. Rudman United States Courthouse
55 Pleasant Street, Room 110
Concord, NH 03301

Puerto Rico:

Federico Degetau Federal Building
150 Carlos Chardon Avenue, Room 150
San Juan, PR 00918

Rhode Island:

Federal Building and United States Courthouse
One Exchange Terrace
Providence, RI 02903-1270

Second Circuit:

Connecticut:

Brien McMahon Federal Building and United States Courthouse
915 Lafayette Boulevard, Room 400
Bridgeport, CT 06604-4706

Abraham Ribicoff Federal Building and United States Courthouse
450 Main Street, Room A-12
Hartford, CT 06103-3022

Richard C. Lee United States Courthouse
141 Church Street, Room 214
New Haven, CT 06510

Eastern District of New York:

Theodore Roosevelt United States Courthouse
225 Cadman Plaza East, Room 1185
Brooklyn, NY 11201-1818

Alfonse M. D'Amato United States Courthouse
Federal Plaza, Room 100
Central Islip, NY 11722

Northern District of New York:

James T. Foley United States Courthouse
445 Broadway, Room 509
Albany, NY 12207

Federal Building
15 Henry Street, 2nd F l o or
Binghamton, NY 13901

14 Durkee Street, 3rd F l o or
Plattsburgh, NY 12901

James M. Hanley Federal Building
100 South Clinton Street, 7th F l o or
Syracuse, NY 13261-6100

Alexander Pirnie Federal Building
10 Broad Street, 3rd Floor
Utica, NY 13501

Southern District of New York:

Daniel Patrick Moynihan United States Courthouse
500 Pearl Street, Room 120
New York, NY 10007-1312

Charles L. Brieant Jr, United States Courthouse
300 Quarropas Street
White Plains, NY 10601-4150

Western District of New York:

United States Courthouse
2 Niagara Square, Room 200
Buffalo, NY 14202

Kenneth B. Keating Federal Building
100 State Street, Room 2120
Rochester, NY 14614

Vermont:

United States Post Office and Courthouse (street address)
204 Main Street, Room 201
Brattleboro, VT 05301
U.S. District Court (mailing address)
P.O. Box 998
Brattleboro, VT 05301

U.S. District Court (street address)
Federal Building
11 Elmwood Avenue, Room 506
Burlington, VT 05401

U.S. District Court (mailing address)
P.O. Box 945
Burlington, VT 05402-0945

United States Post Office and Courthouse (street address)
151 West Street, 2nd F l o or
Rutland, VT 05701

U.S. District Court (mailing address)
P.O. Box 607
Rutland, VT 05701

Third Circuit:

Delaware:

J. Caleb Boggs Federal Building
844 North King Street, 4th Floor
Wilmington, DE 19801-3519

New Jersey:

Mitchell H. Colon United States Courthouse
400 Cooper Street, Room 1050
Camden, NJ 08102-1570

Martin Luther King, Jr. Federal Building
and United States Courthouse
50 Walnut Street, Room 4015
Newark, NJ 07102

Clarkson S. Fisher Federal Building and
United States Courthouse

402 East State Street, Room 2020
Trenton, NJ 08608-1507

Eastern District of Pennsylvania:

Edward N. Cahn Federal Building
and United States Courthouse
504 West Hamilton Street Room 1601
Allentown, PA 18101-1502

Holmes Building
101 Larry Holmes Drive, 4th Floor
Easton, PA 18042

James A. Byrne United States Courthouse
601 Market Street, Room 2609
Philadelphia, PA 19106-1729

Madison Building
400 Washington Street, Room 401
Reading, PA 19601-3915

Middle District of Pennsylvania:

Ronald Reagan Federal Building (street address)
228 Walnut Street
Harrisburg, PA 17108-9998

P.O. Box 983 (mailing address)
Harrisburg, PA 17108-9998

William J. Nealon Federal Building and
United States Courthouse (street address)
235 North Washington Avenue, Room 101
Scranton, PA 18503

P.O. Box 1148 (mailing address)
Scranton, PA 18503

Max Rosenn United States Courthouse
197 South Main Street, Suite 161
Wilkes-Barre, PA 18701-1500

Herman T. Schneebeli Federal Building
240 West Third Street, Suite 218
Williamsport, PA 17701-6412

Western District of Pennsylvania:

17 South Park Row, Room A-150
Erie, PA 16501

Penn Traffic Building
319 Washington Street, Room 208
Johnstown, PA 15901

United States Post Office and Courthouse
700 Grant Street, Room 3110
Pittsburgh, PA 15219-1906

Virgin Islands:

Almeric L. Christian Federal Building
3013 Estate Golden Rock, Room 219
St. Croix, VI 00820

Ron de Lugo Federal Building
5500 Veterans Drive, 3rd Floor
St. Thomas, VI 00802-6424

Fourth Circuit:

Maryland:

Edward A. Garmatz Federal Building and
United States Courthouse
101 West Lombard Street, Room 4415
Baltimore, MD 21201-2605

U n i t e d States Courthouse
6500 Cherry wood Lane, Suite 200
Greenbelt, MD 20770

Maude R. Toulson Federal Building
209 East Main Street
Salisbury, MD 21801-4920

Eastern District of North Carolina:

United States Courthouse
201 South Evans Street, Room 209

Greenville, NC 27858-1121

United States Post Office and Courthouse
413 Middle Street, Room 207
New Bern, NC 28560

Terry Sanford Federal Building (street address)
310 New Bern Avenue, Room 574
Raleigh, NC 27601-1418

P.O. Box 25670 (mailing address)
Raleigh, NC 27601-1418

Alton Lennon Federal Building
Two Princes Street, 2nd F l o or
Wilmington, NC 28401-3947

Middle District of North Carolina:

United States Post Office and Courthouse
323 East Chapel Hill Street, Room 2
Durham, NC 27701-3351

L. Richardson Preyer Federal Building

324 West Market Street, Suite 1
Greensboro, NC 27401-2513

Hiram H. Ward Federal Building
and United States Courthouse
251 North Main Street, Suite 2
Winston Salem, NC 27101

Western District of Carolina:

United States Courthouse
100 Otis Street, Room 309
Asheville, NC 28801-2611

Charles R. Jonas Federal Building
401 West Trade Street, Room 210
Charlotte, NC 28202

United States Post Office
200 West Broad Street, Room 304
Statesville, NC 28677

South Carolina:

Hollings Judicial Center
83 Meeting Street
Charleston, SC 29401

Matthew J. Perry Jr., United States Courthouse
901 Richland Street
Columbia, SC 29201

John L. McMillan Federal Building and
United States Courthouse
401 West Evans Street
Florence, SC 29501

C.F. Haynsworth Federal Building and
United States Courthouse
300 East Washington Street
Greensville, SC 29601

Eastern District of Virginia:

Albert V. Bryan United States Courthouse
401 Courthouse Square, 2nd F l o or
Alexandria, VA 22314-5704

Washington Building
100 Riverside Parkway
Fredericksburg, VA 22406

United States Courthouse
2400 West Avenue, 1st Floor
Newport News, VA 23607

Walter E. Hoffman United States Courthouse
600 Granby Street, Room 193
Norfolk, VA 23510-1915

Spotswood W. Robinson III and Robert R. Merhige, Jr.
United States Courthouse
701 East Broad Street,, Suite 3000
Richmond, VA 2321

Western District of Virginia:

Federal Building

72

180 West Main Street, Room 104
Abingdon, VA 24210

C. Bascom Slemp Federal Building (street address)
322 East Wood Avenue, Room 301
Big Stone Gap, VA 24219-2861

P.O. Box 209 (mailing address)
Big Stone Gap, VA 24219-2861

United States Courthouse
255 West Main Street, Room 304
Charlottesville, VA 22902-5047

Dan Daniel United States Post Office (street address) 700 Main Street, Room 202
Danville, VA 24541-1819

P.O. Box 1400 (mailing address)
Danville, VA 24541-1819
United States Courthouse
116 North Main Street, Room 314
Harrisonburg, VA 22802

United States Courthouse
1101 Court Street, Room A66
Lynchburg, VA 24504-4503

Richard H. Poff Federal Building (street address) 210 Franklin Road, S.W., Room 308
Roanoke, VA 24011-2204

P.O. Box 1234 (mailing address)
Roanoke, VA 24011-2204

Northern District of West Virginia:

United States Post Office (street address)
500 West Pike Street, Suite 301
Clarksburg, WV 26301

P.O. Box 2808 (mailing address)
Clarksburg, WV 26301

Jennings Randolph Federal Center (street address)
300 Third Street, Suite 227
Elikins, WV 26241

P.O. Box 1518 (mailing address)
Elkins, WV 26241

Federal Building
217 West King Street, 1st Floor
Martinsburg, WV 25401

Federal Building and United States Courthouse (street address)
1125 Chapline Street, Suite 247
Wheeling, WV 26003

P.O. Box 471 (mailing address)
Wheeling, WV 26003

Southern District of West Virginia:

Robert C. Byrd United States Courthouse and
IRS Complex
110 North Heber Street, Room 119
Beckley, WV 25801

Elizabeth Kee Federal Building
601 Federal Street, Room 2303
Bluefield, WV 24701

Robert C Byrd United States Courthouse
300 Virginia Street East, Room 2400
Charleston, WV 25301

Sidney L. Christie Federal Building
845 Fifth Avenue, Room 101
Huntington, WV 25701-2014

Federal Building
425 Juliana Street, Room 5102
Parkersburg, WV 26101

Fifth Circuit:

Eastern District of Louisiana:

Hale Boggs Federal Building and
United States Courthouse
500 Poydras Street, Room C-151
New Orleans, LA 70130

Middle District of Louisiana:

Russell B. Long Federal Building
777 Florida Street, Suite 139

Baton Rouge, LA 70801

Western District of Louisiana:

United States Post Office and Courthouse
515 Murray Street, Room 105
Alexandria, LA 71301

United States Courthouse
800 Lafayette Street, Suite 2100
Lafayette, LA 70501

Edwin F. Hunter, Jr. United States Courthouse
and Federal Building
611 Broad Street, Suite 188
Lake Charles, LA 70602

Federal Building (street address)
201 Jackson Street, Suite 215
Monroe, LA 71201

P.O. Box 3087 (mailing address)
Monroe, LA 71201

United States Courthouse
300 Fannin Street, Suite 1167
Shreveport, LA 71101

Northern District of Mississippi:

T.G. Abernethy Federal Building (street address)
301 West Commerce Street, Room 310
Aberdeen, MS 39730

P.O. Box 704 (mailing address)
Aberdeen, MS 39730

Federal Building (street address)
305 Main Street, Room 329
Greensville, MS 38701

P.O. Box 190 (mailing address)
Greensville, MS 38701

Federal Building and United States Courthouse
911 Jackson Avenue East, Room 369
Oxford, MS 38655

Southern District of Mississippi:

Dan M. Russell, Jr. United States Courthouse
2012 15th Street, Room 403
Gulfport, MS 39501

United States Courthouse and Federal Building
701 North Main Street, Room 200
Hattiesburg, MS 39401

United States Courthouse
501 East Court Street, Suite 2.500
Jackson, MS 39201-2409

United States Courthouse
109 South Pearl Street, 2nd F l o or
Natchez, MS 39120-3466

Eastern District of Texas:

Jack Brooks Federal Building
and United States Courthouse
300 Willow Street
Beaumont, TX 77701

Ward R. Burke United States Courthouse
104 North Third Street
Lufkin, TX 75901

Sam B. Hall J. Federal Building and
United States Courthouse
100 East Houston Street
Marshall, TX 75670-4144

United States Courthouse
7940 Preston Road
Piano, TX 75024

Federal Building
101 East Pecan Street, 1st Floor
Sherman, TX 75090

United States Courthouse and Post Office
500 North State Line Avenue, 3rd F l o or
Texarkana, TX 71854-5957

William M. Steger Federal Building

and United States Courthouse
211 West Ferguson Street, Room 106
Tyler, TX 75702

Northern District of Texas:

United States Post Office and Courthouse
341 Pine Street, Room 2008
Abilene, TX 79601

J. Marvin James Federal Building
205 East Fifth Avenue, Room 103
Amarillo, TX 79101

Earle Cabell Federal Building
and United States Courthouse
1100 Commerce Street, Room 1452
Dallas, TX 75242

Eldon B. Mahon United States Courthouse
501 West Tenth Street, Room 310
Fort Worth, TX 76102

George H. Mahon Federal Building
1205 Texas Avenue, Room 209
Lubbock, TX 79401

O.C. Fisher Federal Building and United States Courthouse
33 East Twohig Avenue, Room 202
San Angelo, TX 76901

United States Post Office and Courthouse
1000 Lamar Street, Room 203
Wichita falls, TX 76301

Southern District of Texas:

Federal Building and United States Courthouse
600 East Harrison Street, Room 1158
Brownsville, TX 78520

United States Courthouse
1133 North Shoreline Boulevard, Room 208
Corpus Christi, TX 78401

United States Courthouse (street address)
601 25th Street

Galveston, TX 77550

P.O. Box 2300 (mailing address)
Galveston, TX 77550

Bob Casey United States Courthouse (street address)
515 Rusk Street, Room 5300
Houston, TX 77002-2600

P.O. Box 61010 (mailing address)
Houston, TX 77002-2600

United States Courthouse
1300 Victoria Street, 1st Floor
Laredo, TX 78040

Bentsen Tower
1701 West Business Highway 83, Room 1011
McAllen, TX 78501

Martin Luther King United States Post Office
and Courthouse
312 South Main Street, Room 406
Victoria TX 77901

Western District of Texas:

United States Courthouse
2450 North Highway 118, 1 s t F l o or
Alpine, TX 79830-2026

United States Courthouse
501 West 5 t h Street
Austin, TX 78701

United States Courthouse
111 East Broadway Street, Room L1OO
Del Rio, TX 78840

Albert Armendariz, Sr. United States Courthouse
525 Magoffin Avenue, Room 105
E l Paso, TX 79901

George H.W. Bush and George W. Bush United States
Courthouse and George Mahon Federal Building
200 East Wall Street, Room 107
Midland, TX 79701

Lucius D. Bunton, III United States Courthouse
410 South Cedar Street, 1st Floor
Pecos, TX 79772

John H. Wood, Jr. United States Courthouse
655 East Durango Boulevard, Room G-65
San Antonio, TX 78206

United States Courthouse
800 Franklin Avenue, 3rd Floor
Waco, TX 76701

Sixth Circuit:

Eastern District of Kentucky:

Carl D. Perkins Federal Building
1405 Greenup Avenue, 3rd Floor
Ashland, KY 41101-7542

United States Courthouse
35 West Fifth Street, 2nd Floor
Covington, KY 41011

John C. Watts Federal Building
330 West Broadway, 3rd Floor
Frankfort, KY 40601-1922

United States Courthouse and Post Office
101 Barr Street, 2nd Floor
Lexington, KY 40507-1313

London Courthouse Annex
310 South Main Street, 1st Floor
London, KY 40741

Federal Building
110 Main Street, 2nd F l o or
Pikeville, KY 41501-1163

Western District of Kentucky:

Federal Building
241 East Main Street, Room 120
Bowling Green KY 42101-2141

Gene Snyder United States Courthouse
601 West Broadway, Suite 106
Louisville, KY 40202-2238

Federal Building
432 Frederica Street, Room 126
Owensboro, KY 42301-3013

Federal Building
501 Broadway Street, Room 127
Paducah KY 42001-6856

Eastern District of Michigan:

Federal Building (street address)
200 East Liberty Street, Room 120
Ann Arbor, MI 48104

P.O. Box 8199 (mailing address)
Ann Arbor, MI 48104

United States Post Office (street address)
1000 Washington Avenue, Room 304
Bay City, MI 48706

Theodore Levin United States Courthouse
231 West Lafayette Boulevard, 5th Floor
Detroit, MI 48226

Federal Building
600 Church Street, 1st Floor
Flint, MI 48502

Western District of Michigan:

Gerald R. Ford Federal Building
110 Michigan Street, N.W., Room 399
Grand Rapids, MI 49503

Federal Building
410 West Michigan Avenue, Room B-35
Kalamazoo, MI 49007

Federal Building
315 West Allegan Street, Room 113
Lansing, MI 48933-1528

United States Post Office and Courthouse
202 West Washington Street, Room 229
Marquette, MI 49855-4036

Northern District of Ohio:

John F. Seiberling Federal Building
and United States Courthouse
Two South Main Street, Room 568
Akron, OH 44308

Carl B. Stokes United States Courthouse
801 West Superior Avenue
Cleveland, OH 44113

James M. Ashley and Thomas W.L. Ashley
United States Courthouse
1716 Spielbusch Avenue, Room 114
Toledo, OH 43604

Thomas D. Lambros Federal Building
and United States Courthouse
125 Market Street, Room 337
Youngstown, OH 44503

Southern District of Ohio:

Potter Stewart United States Courthouse
100 East Fifth Street, Room 103
Cincinnati, OH 45202

Joseph P. Kinneary United States Courthouse
85 Marconi Boulevard, Room 121
Columbus, OH 43215

United States Courthouse and Federal Building
200 West Second Street, Room 712
Dayton, OH 45402

Eastern District of Tennessee:

Joel W. Solomon Federal Building
and United States Courthouse
900 Georgia Avenue, Room 309
Chattanooga, TN 37402

James H. Quillen United States Courthouse
220 West Depot Street, Suite 200
Greenville, TN 37743

Howard H. Baker Jr. United States Courthouse
800 Market Street, Suite 130
Knoxvillle, TN 37902

United States Post Office and Courthouse
200 South Jefferson Street, Room 201
Winchester, TN 37398

Middle District of Tennessee:

Estes Kefauver Federal Building
and United States Courthouse
801 Broadway, Room 800
Nashville, TN 37203-3816

Western District of Tennessee:

United States Courthouse
111 South Highland Avenue, Room 262
Jackson, TN 38301

Clifford Davis and Odell Horton Federal Building
167 North Main Street, Room 242
Memphis, TN 38103

Seventh Circuit:

Central District of Illinois:

Federal Building
100 N.E. Monroe Street, Room 309
Peoria, IL 61602

United States Courthouse
211 19th Street, Room 203
Rock Island, IL 61201

Paul Findley Federal Building
and United States Courthouse
600 East Monroe Street, Room 151
Springfield, IL 62701

United States Courthouse
201 South Vine Street, Room 218
Urbana, IL 61801

Northern District of Illinois:

Everett McKinley Dirksen United States Courthouse
219 South Dearborn Street, 20th Floor
Chicago, IL 60604

Stanley J. Roszkowski United States Courthouse
327 South Church Street
Rockford, IL 61101

Southern District of Illinois:

United States Courthouse
301 West Main Street, 1st Floor
Benton, IL 62812

Melvin Price Federal Building
and United States Courthouse
750 Missouri Avenue, Room 104
East St. Louis, IL 62201

Northern District of Indiana:

E. Ross Adair Federal Building
and United States Courthouse
1300 South Harrison Street, Room 1108
Fort Wayne, IN 46802

United States Courthouse
5400 Federal Plaza, Suite 2300
Hammond, IN 46320

Charles A. Halleck Federal Building (street address)
230 North Fourth Street, Room 214
Lafayette, IN 47901

P.O. Box 1340 (mailing address)
Lafayette, IN 47901

Robert A. Grant Federal Building
and United States Courthouse

204 South Main Street, Room 102
South Bend, IN 46601

Southern District of Indiana:

Federal Building
101 N.W. Martin Luther King Jr. Boulevard, Room 304
Evansville, IN 47708-1951

Birch Bayh Federal Building
and United States Courthouse
46 East Ohio Street, Room 105
Indianapolis, IN 46204

Lee H. Hamilton Federal Building
and United States Courthouse
121 West Spring Street, Room 210
New Albany, IN 47150

United States Courthouse
921 Ohio Street, Room 104
Terre Haute, IN 47801

Eastern District of Wisconsin:

Jefferson Court Building
125 South Jefferson Street, Room 102
Green Bay, WI 54301

United States Courthouse and Federal Building
517 East Wisconsin Avenue, Room 362
Milwaukee, WI 53202

Western District of Wisconsin:

Robert W. Kastenmeier United States Courthouse
120 North Henry Street, Room 320
Madison, WI 53703-2559

Eighth Circuit:

Eastern District of Arkansas:

Federal Building
615 South Main Street, Room 312
Jonesboro, AR 72401

Richard Sheppard Arnold United States Courthouse
600 West Capitol Avenue, Room A149
Little Rock, AR 72201

George Howard, Jr. Federal Building
and United States Courthouse
100 East Eighth Avenue, Room 205
Pine Bluff, AR 71601

Western District of Arkansas:

United States Post Office and Courthouse
101 South Jackson Avenue, Room 205
El Dorado, AR 71730

John Paul Hammerschmidt Federal Building
35 East Mountain Street, Room 510
Fayetteville, AR 72701

Judge Isaac C. Parker Federal Building
30 South Sixth Street, Room 1038
Fort Smith, AR 72901

United States Courthouse and Post Office Building
500 North State Line Avenue, Room 302
Texarkana, AR 75501

Northern District of Iowa:

United States Courthouse (street address)
111 Seventh Avenue, S.E., 5th Floor
Cedar Rapids, IA 52401-2101

Internal Box 12 (mailing address)
Cedar Rapids, IA 52401-2101

United States Courthouse
320 Sixth Street, Room 301
Sioux City, IA 51101-1210

Southern District of Iowa:

United States Post Office and Courthouse (street address)
8 South Sixth Street, Room 313
Council Bluffs, IA 51501-4200

P.O. Box 307 (mailing address)
Council Bluffs, IA 51501-4200

United States Courthouse
131 East Fourth Street
Davenport, IA 52801-1516

United States Courthouse (street address)
123 East Walnut Street, Room 300
Des Moines, IA 50309-2035

P.O. Box 9344 (mailing address)
Des Moines, IA 50309-2035

Minnesota:

Gerald W. Heaney Federal Building
and United States Courthouse
515 West First Street, Room 417
Duluth, MN 55802

United States Courthouse
118 South Mill Street, Room 205
Fergus Falls, MN 56537

United States Courthouse
300 South Fourth Street, Suite 202
Minneapolis, MN 55415

Warren E. Burger Federal Building
316 North Robert Street
St. Paul, MN 55101

Eastern District of Missouri:

Rush Hudson Limbaugh, Sr. United States Courthouse
555 Independence Street, 2nd Floor
Cape Girardeau, MO 63703-6235

Thomas F. Eagleton United States Courthouse
111 South Tenth Street, Room 3.300
St. Louis, MO 63102-1116

Western District of Missouri:

Christopher S. Bond United States Courthouse
80 Lafayette Street
Jefferson City, MO 65101-1557

Charles Evan Whittaker United States Courthouse
400 East Ninth Street, Room 1510
Kansas City, MO 64106

United States Courthouse
222 North John Q. Hammons Parkway, Room 1400
Springfield, MO 65806-2515

North Dakota:

Federal Building and United States Courthouse (street address)
220 East Rosser Avenue, Room 476
Bismarck, ND 58501

P.O. Box 1193 (mailing address)
Bismarck. ND 58501

Quentin N. Burdick United States Courthouse
655 First Avenue North, Room 130
Fargo, ND 58102

Nebraska:

Robert V. Denney United States Courthouse
100 Centennial Mall North, Room 593
Lincoln, NE 68508-3803

Roman L. Hruska United States Courthouse
111 South 18th Plaza, Suita 1152
Omeha, NE 68102

South Dakota:

United States Post Office and Courthouse
225 South Pierre Street, Room 405
Pierre, SD 57501

Federal Building and United States Courthouse
515 Ninth Street, Room 302
Rapid City, SD 55701

United States Courthouse
400 South Phillips Avenue, Room 128
Sioux Falls, SD 57104-6851

Ninth Circuit:

Alaska:

Federal Building and United States Courthouse (street address)
222 West 7th Avenue
Anchorage, AK 99513-7500

Internal Box 4 (mailing address)
Anchorage, AK 99513-7500

Federal Building and United States Courthouse (street address)
101 12th Avenue, Room 332
Fairbanks, AK 99701-6236

Internal Box 1 (mailing address)
Fairbanks, AK 99701-6236

Hurff A. Saunders Federal Building (street address)
709 West Ninth Street, Room 979
Juneau, AK 99801-1807

Federal Building
648 Mission Street, Room 507
Ketchikan, AK 99901-6534

United States Post Office and Courthouse (street address)
940 East Front Street
Nome, AK 99762

P.O. Box 130 (mailing address)
Nome, AK 99762

Arizona:

United States Courthouse
123 North San Francisco Street, Suite 200
Flagstaff, AZ 86001-5296

Sandra Day O'Connor United States Courthouse
401 West Washington Street, Room 130
Phoenix, AZ 85003

Evo A. DeConcini United States Courthouse
405 West Congress Street
Tuscon, AZ 85701

Central District of California:

United States Courthouse
312 North Spring Street, Room G-8
Los Angeles, CA 90012-4701

George E. Brown, Jr. United States Courthouse
3470 Twelfth Street, 1st Floor
Riverside, CA 92501-3801

Ronald Reagan Federal Building
and United States Courthouse
411 West Fourth Street, Room 1-053
Santa Ana, CA 92701

Federal Public Defender
321 East Second Street
Los Angeles, CA 90012-4206

Eastern District of California:

510 19th Street, Suite 200
Bakersfield, CA 93301-4641

Robert E. Coyle United States Courthouse
2500 Tulare Street, Room 1501
Fresno, CA 93721

2986 Bechelli Lane
Redding, CA 96002-1903

Robert T. Matsui United States Courthouse
501 I Street, Room 4-200
Sacramento, CA 95814-7300

Yosemite National Park Courthouse (street address)
Yosemite Village
Yosemite Natl. Park, CA 95389

P.O. Box 575 (mailing address)
Yosemite Natl. Park, CA 95389

Federal Public Defender
801 I Street, 3rd Floor
Sacramento, CA 95814-2510

Northern District of California:

Federal Building (street address)
514 H Street
Eureka, CA 95501

P.O. Box 1306 (mailing address)
Eureka, CA 95501

Ronald V. Dellums Federal Building
1301 Clay Street, Suite 400S
Oakland, CA 94612-5217

Phillip Burton United States Courthouse (street address)
450 Golden Gate Avenue, 16th Floor
San Francisco, CA 94102-3434

Internal Box 36060 (mailing address)
San Francisco, CA 94102-3434

Robert F. Peckham Federal Building
and United States Courthouse
280 South First Street, Room 2112
San Jose, CA 95113-3002

Federal Public Defender
555 Twelfth Street, Suite 650
Oakland, Ca 94607

South District of California:

United States Courthouse
2003 West Adams Avenue, 1st Floor
El Centro, CA 92243

United States Courthouse (Annex)
333 West Broadway, Suite 4290
San Diego, CA 92101

Guam:

United States Courthouse
520 West Soledad Avenue, 4th Floor
Hagatna, GU 96910-4950

Hawaii:

Prince Kuhio Federal Building
300 Ala Moana Boulevard, Room C338
Honolulu, HI 96850-0001

Idaho:

James A. McClure Federal Building
and United States Courthouse
550 West Fort Street, Room 400
Boise, ID 83724-0101

United States Courthouse
6450 North Mineral Drive, Room 149
Coeur d'Alene, ID 83815

Federal Building and United States Courthouse
801 East Sherman Street, Room 199
Pocatello, ID 83201-5730

Northern Mariana Islands:

Horiguchi Building (street building)
123 Kopa Di Oru Street, Room 205
Saipan, MP 96950-0687

P.O. Box 500687 (mailing address)
Saipan, MP 96950-0687

Montana:

James F. Battin United States Courthouse
316 North 26th Street
Billings, MT 59101

Mike Mansfield Federal Building
and United States Courthouse
400 North Main Street
Butte, MT 59701

Missouri River Courthouse
125 Central Avenue West, Suite 110
Great Falls, MT 59404

Paul G. Hatfield United States Courthouse
901 Front Street, Suite 2100
Helena, MT 59626-9708

Russell E. Smith Federal Building (street address)
201 East Broadway Street, Suite 310
Missoula, MT 59802

P.O. Box 8537 (mailing address)
Missoula, MT 59802

Nevada:

Lloyd D. George United States Courthouse
333 Las Vegas Boulevard South, 1st Floor
Las Vegas, NV 89101-7065

Bruce R. Thompson United States Courthouse
and Federal Building
400 South Virginia Street, Room 301
Reno, NV 89501-2193

Oregon:

Wayne Lyman Morse United States Courthouse
405 East Eighth Avenue, Room 2100
Eugene, OR 97401-2705

James A. Redden United States Courthouse
310 West Sixth Street, Room 201
Medford, OR 97501-2766

Mark O. Hatfield United States Courthouse
1000 Southwest Third Avenue, Room 740
Portland, OR 97204-2802

Eastern District of Washington:

Federal Building
825 Jadwin Avenue, Suite 174
Richland, WA 99352-3589

Thomas S. Foley United States Courthouse
920 West Riverside Avenue, Suite 840
Spokane, WA 99201-1010

William O. Douglas Federal Building
25 South Third Street, 2nd Floor
Yakima, WA 98901-2742

Western District of Washington:

United States Courthouse
700 Stewart Street, Room 2310
Seattle, WA 98101-1271

United States Courthouse
1717 Pacific Avenue, Room 3100
Tacoma, WA 98402-3234

Tenth Circuit:

Colorado:

Alfred A. Arraj United States Courthouse
90119th Street, 2nd Floor
Denver, CO 80202-3660

Kansas:

Robert J. Dole United States Courthouse
500 State Avenue, Room 259
Kansas City, KS 66101-2400

Fran Carlson Federal Building
and United States Courthouse
444 Southeast Quincy Street, Room 490
Topeka, KS 66683

United States Courthouse
401 North Market Street, Room 204
Wichita, KS 67202-2000

New Mexico:

Pete V. Domenici United States Courthouse
333 Lomas Boulevard, N.W> Suite 270
Albuquerque, NM 87102

U.S. District Courthouse
100 North Church Street Room 2
Las Cruces, NM 88001

Santiago E. Campos United States Courthouse
106 South Federal Place
Santa Fe, NM 87501-1902

Eastern District of Oklahoma:

Ed Edmondson United States Courthouse (street address)
101 North Fifth Street
Muskogee, OK 74401-6205

P.O. Box 607 (mailing address)
Muskogee, OK 74401-6205

Northern District of Oklahoma:

Page Belcher Federal Building
and United States Courthouse
333 West Fourth Street, Room 411
Tulsa, OK 74103-3819

Western District of Oklahoma:

United States Courthouse
200 Northwest Fourth Street, Room 1210
Oklahoma City, OK 73102

United States Courthouse
410 Southwest Fifth Street, Room 207
Lawton, OK 73501-4628

Utah:

Frank E. Moss United States Courthouse
350 South Main Street, Room 150
Salt Lake City, UT 84101

Wyoming:

Ewing T. Kerr Federal Building
and United States Courthouse
111 South Wolcott, Street, 1st Floor
Casper, WY 82601

Joseph C. O'Mahoney Federal Building
2120 Capitol Avenue, Room 2141
Cheyenne, WY 82001

Yellowstone Justice Center (street address)
1001 Mammoth Esplanade, Mammoth Hot Springs
Yellowstone Natl. Park, WY 82190

P.O. Box 387 (mailing address)
Yellowstone Natl. Park, WY 82190

Eleventh Circuit:

Middle District of Alabama:

Frank M. Johnson, Jr. Federal Courthouse Annex
One Church Street, Suite B-110
Montgomery, AL 36104

Northern District of Alabama:

Hugo L. Black United States Courthouse
1729 Fifth Avenue North, Room 140
Birmingham, AL 35203-2000

United States Post Office and Courthouse
101 Holmes Avenue, N.E., 1st Floor
Huntsville, AL 35801

Tuscaloosa Federal Courthouse
2005 University Boulevard
Tuscaloosa, AL 35401

Southern District of Alabama:

John A. Campbell United States Courthouse
113 St. Joseph Street, Room 123
Mobile, AL 36602

Middle District of Florida:

United States Courthouse and Federal Building
2110 First Street, Room 2-194
Fort Myers, FL 33901

Bryan Simpson United States Courthouse
300 North Hogan Street, Room 9-150
Jacksonville, FL 33202-4204

Golden-Collum Federal Building
and United States Courthouse
207 Northwest Second Street, Suite 337
Ocala, FL 34475-6603

United States Courthouse
401 West Central Boulevard, Suite 1200
Orlando, FL 32801

Sam M. Gibbons United States Courthouse
801 North Florida Avenue, 2nd Floor
Tampa, FL 33602

Northern District of Florida:

Federal Building
401 Southeast First Avenue, Room 243
Gainesville, FL 32601

Gulf Coast Building
30 West Government Street, 2nd Floor
Panama City, FL 32401

United States Courthouse
One North Palafox Street, 2nd Floor
Pensacola, FL 32502

United States Courthouse Annex
111 North Adams Street, 3rd Floor
Tallahassee, FL 32301

Southern District of Florida:

United States Courthouse
299 East Broward Boulevard, Room 108
Fort Lauderdale, FL 33301

Alto Lee Adams, Sr. United States Courthouse
101 South U.S. Highway 1, Room 1016
Fort Pierce, FL 34950

United States Post Office Courthouse
301 Simonton Street
Miami, FL 33040

Wilkie D. Ferguson, Jr. United States Courthouse
400 North Miami Avenue, Room 8
Miami, FL 33128

Paul G. Rogers Federal Building
and United States Courthouse
701 Clematis Street, Room 402
West Palm Beach, FL 33401

Middle District of Georgia:

C.B. King United States Courthouse
201 West Broad Avenue
Albany, GA 31701-2566

United States Post Office and Courthouse (street address)
115 East Hancock Avenue, 2nd Floor
Athens, GA 30601

P.O. Box 1106 (mailing address)
Athens, GA 30601

United States Post Office and Courthouse (street address)
120 12th Street, Suite 216
Columbus, GA 31902

P.O. Box 124 (mailing address)
Columbus, GA 31902

William Augustus Bootle federal Building
and United States Courthouse (street address)
475 Mulberry Street, Suite 216
Macon, GA 31201

P.O. Box 128 (mailing address)
Macon, GA 31601

United Post Office and Courthouse (street address)
401 North Patterson Street, Suite 212
Valdosta, GA 31601

P.O. Box 68 (mailing address)
Valdosta, GA 31601

Northern District of Georgia:

Richard B. Russell Federal Building
and United States Courthouse
75 Spring Street, S.W., Room 2211
Atlanta, GA 30303

United States Courthouse
121 Spring Street, S.E., Room 201
Gainesville GA 30501

Lewis R. Morgan Federal Building
and United States Courthouse
18 Greenville Street, Room 352
Newnan, GA 30263

United States Courthouse
600 East First Street, Room 304
Rome, GA 30161

Southern District of Georgia:

Federal Justice Center - United States Courthouse
600 James Brown Boulevard
Augusta, GA 30903

Frank M. Scarlett Federal Building
801 Gloucester Street
Brunswick, GA 31520

Tomochichi United States Courthouse (street address)
125 Bull Street, 3rd Floor
Savannah, GA 31402

P.O. Box 8286 (mailing address)
Savannah, GA 31402

District of Columbia Addresses:

District of Columbia Court of Appeals
430 E Street, N.W.
Washington, D.C. 20001

Superior Court of District of Columbia
500 Indiana Avenue, N.W.
Washington, D.C. 20001

A7   Circuit Locations

STATES INCLUDED IN EACH UNITED STATES COURT OF APPEALS

First Circuit: Maine, Massachusetts, New Hampshire, Puerto Rico,
                            Rhode Island

Second Circuit: Connecticut, New York, Vermont.

Third Circuit: Delaware, New Jersey, Pennsylvania, Virgin Islands

Fourth Circuit: Maryland, North Carolina, South Carolina,
                            Virginia, West Virginia

Fifth Circuit: Louisiana, Mississippi, Texas.

Sixth Circuit: Kentucky, Michigan, Ohio, Tennessee.

Seventh Circuit: Illinois, Indiana, Wisconsin.

Eight Circuit: Arkansas, Iowa, Minnesota, Missouri
                            Nebraska, North Dakota, South Dakota.

Ninth Circuit: Alaska, Arizona, California, Hawaii, Idaho,
                            Montana, Nevada, Oregon, Washington, Guam,
                            Northern Mariana Islands

Tenth Circuit: Colorado, Kansas, New Mexico, Oklahoma, Utah.

Eleventh Circuit: Alabama, Florida, Georgia.

D.C. Circuit: The District of Columbia

If you wish to contact the Author, you can write him at

TAWL Foundation

Eric VanBuren

11215 Maiden Drive

Bowie, Md 20716

Made in the USA
San Bernardino, CA
29 February 2016